JOURNEY TO MARS

PUBLISHED BY SMART APPLE MEDIA

123 SOUTH BROAD STREET

MANKATO, MINNESOTA 56001

PHOTOS: NASA/JPL/CALTECH; COVER, PAGE 3—NASA/NSSDC;

PAGE 27—NASA/KENNEDY SPACE CENTER

DESIGN AND PRODUCTION: EVANSDAY DESIGN

LIBRARY OF CONGRESS CATALOGING-IN-PUBLICATION DATA

GAINES, ANN.

JOURNEY TO MARS / BY ANN GRAHAM GAINES AND

ADELE D. RICHARDSON

P. CM. — (ABOVE AND BEYOND)

INCLUDES INDEX.

SUMMARY: DESCRIBES EXPLORATION OF THE PLANET MARS, WITH AN

EMPHASIS ON THE PATHFINDER AND MARS GLOBAL SURVEYOR

SPACECRAFT, WHAT THEY FOUND, AND FUTURE MISSIONS.

ISBN 1-58340-048-6

1. MARS (PLANET)—EXPLORATION—JUVENILE LITERATURE. 2. SPACE FLIGHT TO

MARS—JUVENILE LITERATURE. [1. MARS (PLANET)—

EXPLORATION. 2. SPACE FLIGHT TO MARS.] I. RICHARDSON, ADELE, 1966–.

II. TITLE. III. SERIES: ABOVE AND BEYOND (MANKATO, MINN.)

QB641.G28   1999

919.9'2304—DC21   98-39022

FIRST EDITION

1 3 5 7 9 8 6 4 2

JOURNEY TO MARS

ANN GRAHAM GAINES & ADELE D. RICHARDSON

ABOVE & BEYOND

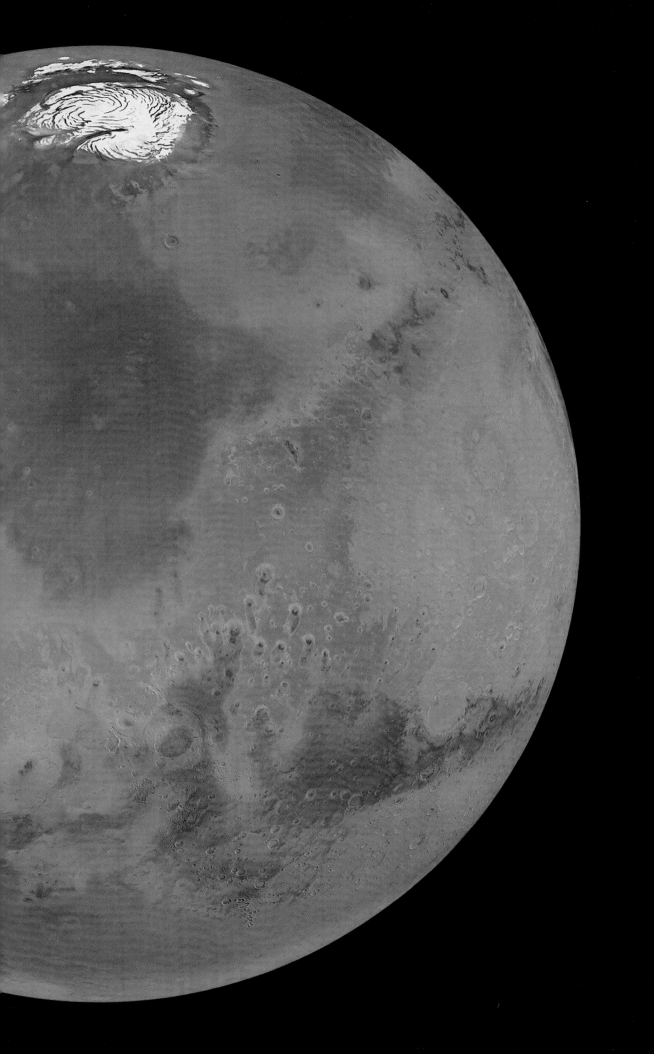

ON DECEMBER 4, 1996, a Delta II rocket carrying

Pathfinder sat poised on a launch pad at the

Kennedy Space Center ✳ The final seconds to

launch ticked away, and the rocket's engines

roared to life in a fiery blaze, pushing *Pathfinder*

away from Earth forever ✳ Within minutes, it

was orbiting the planet ✳ Then another rocket

engine flamed to life with a powerful burst,

hurling *Pathfinder* beyond the pull of Earth's

gravity and into a new orbit around the sun ✳

Over the next seven months, *Pathfinder* traveled

120 million miles (193 million km) before reach-

ing its final destination: Mars ✳

Preparing
Pathfinder

Humans have been fascinated by Mars for centuries—probably ever since someone first spotted its distant light in the night sky. This interest has only intensified in the last half-century. Scientists have debated whether such a planet could support life. Authors have written books about imaginary journeys to the "red planet." Movies have been made portraying contact between humans and "Martians."

The first real attempt to visit Mars began on August 20, 1975. On that date, the National Aeronautics and Space Administration (NASA) launched a spacecraft called *Viking 1*. The spacecraft landed on the surface of Mars on July 20, 1976—nearly one year after its launch. NASA launched *Viking 2* on September 5, 1975. It too took nearly a year to reach Mars, joining *Viking 1* on the planet's surface on September 3, 1976.

These unmanned Mars explorers sent a great deal of information and thousands of pictures back to scientists on Earth. However, they fell far short of satisfying our curiosity about the most Earth-like planet in our solar system.

The Mars Pathfinder Program officially began on May 8, 1992, when NASA announced plans to further explore the red planet. *Pathfinder*'s **mission** would be to study the Martian environment on a much more thorough scale than had been done in the 1970s. NASA engineers also hoped to use *Pathfinder* to prove that a scientific **payload** could be inexpensively built and landed on another planet.

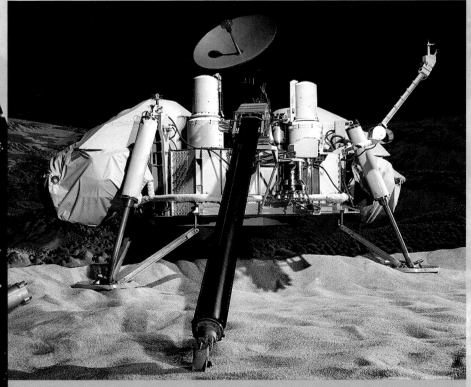

Viking 1, *the first spacecraft to explore the surface of Mars.*

Pathfinder would not be just another **satellite** sent to circle the planet and take pictures. NASA's plans included landing *Pathfinder* on Mars, then using a small, remote-controlled vehicle to explore and study the planet's surface. Computers on *Pathfinder* would send the vehicle's findings back to Earth within minutes.

Teams of scientists and engineers across the United States worked together to design the new spacecraft. Programmers wrote computer software that would let *Pathfinder* communicate with Earth throughout its entire voyage and operation. Teams of engineers then built the individual sections of *Pathfinder*; some teams put together computers, rockets, heat shields, and solar panels, while others built two special pieces of equipment—the **lander** and the **rover**.

A **rover** *is a robotic vehicle built to explore land.*

A **satellite** *is an object—natural or man-made—that orbits a celestial body.*

A **lander** *is a spacecraft designed to land on a celestial body.*

Pathfinder's *rover, named* Sojourner, *performed beyond the expectations of scientists.*

The lander was a small device that weighed just 772 pounds (347 kg) and stood barely 3 feet (1 m) tall. It contained computers, software, and scientific instruments to monitor Martian weather. The lander also contained specially designed cameras that would be used to photograph the Martian landscape, as well as the dust and water vapor in Mars' atmosphere.

Next, workers attached air bags and three large parachutes to the lander to soften its landing on Mars. The entire lander was also covered by heat shields, which would keep the equipment from burning up when the space-craft entered Mars' atmosphere.

The lander also carried a six-wheeled rover named *Sojourner* that was equipped with computers, software, and cameras. Considering its capabilities, *Sojourner* was extremely small—only two feet (60 cm) long, or about the size of an average microwave oven. After the rover's release on Mars, scientists would be able to guide it by sending commands from Earth. But *Sojourner* would also be able to move around by itself without direct instructions. To do this, it would use lasers to "feel" the landscape in front of it and to avoid obstacles such as rocks and crevices.

After reaching Mars, the lander and the rover would operate on solar energy. Because both of its parts would use solar panels to collect the sun's energy, *Pathfinder* would not need fuel on Mars, allowing it to travel much lighter during its journey.

A panoramic image (above and opposite) from the Pathfinder *lander.*

Finally, NASA scientists brought all of the sections together to assemble *Pathfinder*. They tested every piece of equipment repeatedly to make sure it would operate flawlessly. There was little room for error or malfunction. During *Pathfinder*'s seven-month trip, the equipment would have to withstand the deep cold and vacuum of space. Then, while entering the Martian atmosphere, it would have to face the entirely different challenge of intense heat.

Pathfinder sent thousands of incredibly clear photos back to Earth.

Journey
to Mars

During *Pathfinder*'s departure from Earth atop a Delta II rocket, three stages of the rocket flared up and fell away, sending *Pathfinder* on its course. Finally, only the lander itself was left, encased in a metal shell with small rockets to steer the spacecraft.

As *Pathfinder* flew past Earth's moon, its star scanner came alive. This instrument began calculating the spacecraft's exact position in space. Throughout the long trip, the spacecraft's computers continuously sent this information back to scientists at the Jet Propulsion Laboratory in California, who carefully monitored *Pathfinder*'s progress. On four occasions, they adjusted *Pathfinder*'s **trajectory** to keep it on the proper course.

Pathfinder reached speeds of about 17,000 miles (27,400 km) per hour. It traveled more than 408,000 miles (657,600 km) per day, drawing steadily closer to Mars.

Pathfinder's journey through space ended on July 4, 1997. At 10 AM Eastern Daylight Time, *Pathfinder* plunged into the Martian atmosphere, still traveling at 17,000 miles (27,400 km) per hour. As the friction caused by the planet's

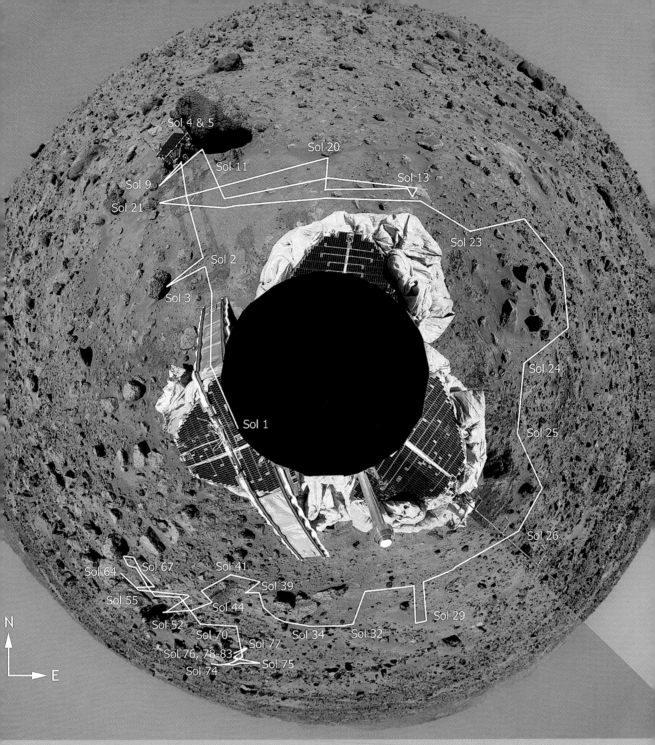

N

E

A **trajectory** is the curved
path of an object in space.

JULY 4, 1997

Scientists receive the first photograph of Mars sent by Pathfinder.

atmosphere heated *Pathfinder*'s metal shell and slowed the spacecraft down, the external heat shields functioned properly, protecting the spacecraft's equipment.

As *Pathfinder* neared Mars' surface, its three large parachutes opened, further slowing the spacecraft. Next, *Pathfinder* released its heat shields, which fell to the planet's surface on their own. As the spacecraft headed toward a landing, it was traveling just 35 miles (56 km) per hour. At a programmed time, *Pathfinder* released its parachutes and the small remaining rockets. Giant air bags 17 feet (5 m) in diameter inflated around the spacecraft in just two seconds.

Just as it reached landing speed, *Pathfinder* collided with the surface of Mars. Its air bags absorbed the impact of the landing, and *Pathfinder* bounced 40 feet (12 m) high before falling back to the ground. During the next 100 seconds, the spacecraft bounced 15 more times before finally rolling to a stop. The air bags then began to deflate, and the three metal pieces that had encased the spacecraft folded down.

Pathfinder had successfully landed on a rocky plain called Ares Villis. There it would receive plenty of sunshine to run its equipment. It was time for Sojourner to begin roving the surface of the mysterious red planet.

Pathfinder's *air bags were vital during the spacecraft's rocky landing.*

Exploring the
Red Planet

Pathfinder's transmitter began sending signals to NASA immediately after the landing. Because Earth is closer to the sun than is Mars, our planet has a tighter orbit around the sun. The Earth's distance from Mars—which has a much larger, slower orbit—varies greatly. Depending on the distance between the two planets, a message can take 4 to 21 minutes to travel from Mars to Earth.

Pathfinder's first message, which reached Earth in just 10 minutes, told scientists that the spacecraft's systems were operating properly. The first image from the lander's camera arrived on Earth shortly afterward. The image showed the Martian landscape, part of the lander, and a partially inflated air bag.

During the next 24 hours, scientists instructed Pathfinder to finish deflating and removing the air bags. The lander then opened a ramp to let Sojourner roll onto the planet's surface. When it hit Martian soil, the rover became the first mobile vehicle ever used on another planet. Within minutes, people on Earth saw pictures of Sojourner on Mars.

In the weeks that followed, instruments on the lander analyzed the Martian climate and atmosphere. Scientists reviewed the photos that Pathfinder sent to Earth and iden-

Sojourner *makes its way across the rocky Martian landscape (left); an image of the beautiful Martian sky (right).*

tified rocks they wanted the rover to study more closely,

guiding *Sojourner* to these rocks by computer instruction.

The rover also carried a **spectrometer** that it used to

study the composition of rocks and soil.

Pathfinder explored Mars for almost three months.

During that time, it sent 2.6 billion **bits** of scientific data—

Bits *are the smallest pieces of information a computer can understand.*

A **spectrometer** *is an instrument used to identify substances by studying the distribution of atoms or molecules.*

including 16,000 images and 15 extensive chemical analyses of rocks and soil—back to Earth. NASA scientists will continue to study this information for years to come.

In its exploration, *Sojourner* found rock samples that contained silicon, a mineral also found in volcanic rock on Earth. Because *Sojourner* found more silicon than scientists had expected, many now believe that Mars once had a number of active volcanoes on its surface.

The area where *Pathfinder* landed also provided evidence that free-flowing water once existed on Mars. From this evidence, scientists believe that a stream hundreds of miles wide passed through Ares Villis. Such a large amount

Like Earth, certain regions of Mars have deep canyons cut into the land.

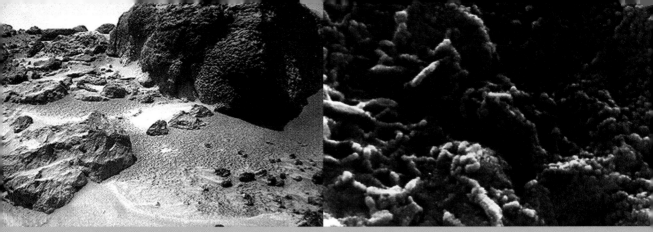

The rugged Martian landscape (left); fossils (right) may hold the key to the red planet's history.

of water suggests that Mars might have been able to support life in its past.

Although scientists lost contact with *Pathfinder* several times while the spacecraft explored Mars, they were able to solve the communications problem each time. On September 27, 1997, however, NASA permanently lost contact with the lander. The lander, which had relayed messages between *Sojourner* and Earth, was no longer functioning; therefore, NASA could no longer receive data from the rover. On March 10, 1998—five and a half months after *Sojourner*'s last contact—NASA announced that *Pathfinder*'s mission was officially over.

As far as scientists can tell, *Sojourner* continues to roam about the Martian landscape using its solar power. No one knows how long it will continue to operate, though eventually it is bound to become damaged and stop functioning. In a sense, the Mars Pathfinder Mission will continue until that day.

Mars
Global Surveyor

Even before the more-publicized Pathfinder Mission was launched, another NASA spacecraft was on its way toward Mars. The *Mars Global Surveyor* was launched on November 7, 1996—one month before *Pathfinder* left Earth. This launch began a decade-long program of **robotic** exploration called the Mars Surveyor Program.

NASA created *Mars Global Surveyor* to replace an earlier spacecraft called *Mars Global Observer*. Scientists lost contact with *Observer* just before it began to orbit Mars in 1993; *Surveyor*'s primary mission was to complete the work *Observer* was unable to do. NASA had hoped that *Surveyor* would send back to Earth more information about Mars than any other vehicle in space history had before. The spacecraft included instruments to create a detailed map of the planet's surface. These instruments were also designed to study the atmosphere, rocks, and soil, and to examine how the planet's polar ice caps change with the seasons. Part of *Surveyor*'s mission was also to help scientists determine once and for all whether life ever existed on Mars.

Scientists were also hoping to learn more about Earth

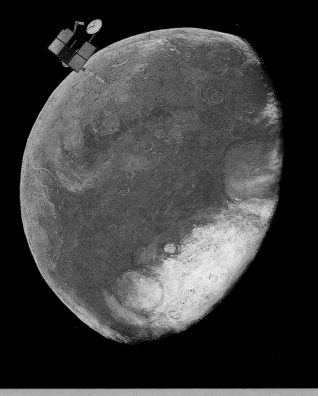

Scientists were left puzzled by Observer's *mysterious disappearance.*

by studying Mars. Drawing comparisons between the two planets could help them better understand Earth's history. It could even help them predict our planet's future. The data provided by *Surveyor* could also help NASA plan future Mars missions and choose future landing sites.

Surveyor was built by engineers and technicians at the Lockheed Martin Astronautics plant in Denver, Colorado. The spacecraft is rectangular in shape and has solar panel "wings" that jut out from the sides. At its launch, *Surveyor* weighed 2,342 pounds (1,060 kg), including its fuel. Most

Robotics *is the branch of science dealing with the design, construction, and operation of robots.*

of this weight is in the box-like center of the spacecraft. This area is actually two units—the **equipment module** and the **propulsion module**—stacked one on top of the other.

Surveyor finally reached Mars on September 11, 1997, more than two months after *Pathfinder* landed on the planet. *Surveyor* then began a 25-minute maneuver called a Mars orbit insertion burn. This maneuver involved firing the spacecraft's rocket engines to slow the vehicle down and place it in a highly **elliptical orbit**.

At first, *Surveyor* needed 48 hours to complete one elliptical orbit around Mars. At its orbital high point, the spacecraft was 34,800 miles (56,000 km) away from the planet's surface; at its low point, *Surveyor* was just 186 miles (300 km) from the surface. Scientists needed to tighten this orbit before the spacecraft would be able to start mapping the planet. To do this, they used a special technique called **aerobraking.** The friction created upon entering the planet's atmosphere also helped to slow the spacecraft. As *Surveyor*'s speed diminished, its orbit tightened, and it gradually flew closer and closer to the planet's surface.

Phase one of aerobraking lasted four months. Scientists

The aerobraking technique used to tighten Surveyor's orbit required precise calculation.

An **equipment module** *contains a spacecraft's electronic and scientific instruments.*

A **propulsion module** *contains a spacecraft's rocket engines and fuel tanks.*

An **elliptical orbit** *is an oval orbit around a celestial body.*

Aerobraking *is the firing of rocket engines to reduce a spacecraft's speed and altitude.*

controlled the aerobraking by computer and made many adjustments to *Surveyor*'s course. Their calculations had to be precisely correct—if *Surveyor*'s orbit took it within 65 miles (105 km) of Mars, the spacecraft could burn up in the atmosphere.

    Surveyor was scheduled to spend one Martian year (about two Earth years) mapping the surface of Mars. This process began in March 1998 and, if all goes according to plan, will end in January 2000. *Surveyor*'s mapping assignment consists of two phases, with a six-month break in between. During the break, scientists will review the data that *Surveyor* has already sent to them.

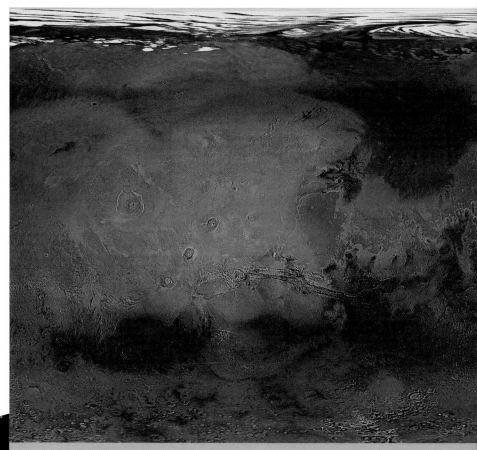

A flattened-out view of the surface of Mars with ice caps visible at the top.

Surveyor's orbit around Mars allows it to pass over the north and south poles of the planet. While on the "day" side of Mars, the side facing the sun, *Surveyor* will always travel southward; on the "night" side, it will always travel northward. NASA scientists designed the orbit path so that instruments aboard *Surveyor* can examine the entire surface of Mars once every 7.2 Earth days.

During the early part of its mission, *Surveyor* performed almost flawlessly. Scientists encountered only one minor problem during aerobraking, when a problem with a solar panel left it out of position when fully extended. After its mission is complete, scientists plan to continue to use *Surveyor* as a communications relay station for future Mars missions until the year 2003 or 2004.

With NASA's technology, orbiting spacecraft can take remarkable photographs.

Future Missions

Because the missions of *Pathfinder* and *Mars Global Surveyor* have been so successful, NASA plans to launch more exploratory spacecraft in the future. Such launches have to be planned very carefully and well in advance: the chance to launch a Mars explorer comes just once every 26 months when the planet is closest to Earth. Mars Surveyor 98, a two-part mission, began in December 1998 with the launching of the *Mars Climate Orbiter*.

Orbiter, which is actually a rebuilt version of the *Mars Global Observer,* was scheduled to reach Mars in September 1999. *Orbiter*'s mission is to study the Martian atmosphere, weather, dust, and water vapor. Like *Surveyor,* it will then serve as a relay station for future communications.

The second part of the Mars Surveyor mission began on January 3, 1999, with the launch of the *Mars Polar Lander*. If the mission goes according to plan, *Lander* will reach Mars early in December 1999. It is slated to land at the south pole of the planet, where it will perform an interesting scientific experiment.

Lander will carry two tiny microprobes that will detach from the spacecraft before it enters Mars' atmosphere. They will slam into the planet's surface at a speed of up to 650 feet (200 m) per second, burrowing about six and a half feet (2 m) into the ground. These probes will determine whether underground ice is present, helping scientists determine if life could have existed on Mars.

The Mars Surveyor 2001 Program will include the launch

All equipment for the Mars Surveyor 98 mission was repeatedly tested before launch.

of an **orbiter,** a lander, and a rover. NASA plans to launch the orbiter in March 2001; it is scheduled to arrive on Mars in December of the same year. It too will map the surface of the planet and serve as a communications relay station. Scientists will compare data from the different missions to determine how the planet has changed from one mission to the next. The lander and rover for this program are scheduled for launch in April 2001 and should arrive on Mars in January 2002. This rover will do more than just explore the planet's surface—it will use a coring drill and container to obtain and store samples for future study.

Mars Surveyor 2003 will be equipped with a long-range, sample-collecting rover. This vehicle will travel farther and collect more samples than the previous rover. Scientists will study the information it provides in their ongoing search for evidence of life on Mars.

NASA is planning another breakthrough mission for the year 2005, when the *Mars Sample Return (MSR)* spacecraft is scheduled for launch. If it successfully serves its purpose, the *MSR* will collect the samples stored by the rovers

An **orbiter** *is a spacecraft designed to orbit a moon or planet.*

The Mars Surveyor 2001 *spacecraft will be an upgraded version of* Pathfinder.

that landed in 2001 and 2003. It will then bring the samples back to Earth in 2008, allowing scientists to study Martian rocks and soil in a laboratory on Earth for the first time.

Other future missions may involve sending astronauts to live and work in a base on Mars. These missions, however, are still simply ideas that will require years of planning and research. Sending humans to Mars would be an expensive, complex, and dangerous undertaking. When NASA does establish a base beyond Earth, the first site will probably be the moon.

Today, Mars is no longer as mysterious as it once was. The *Pathfinder* and *Surveyor* missions have provided us with a wealth of information about the red planet. Scientists will study this data for decades, but that is just the beginning of our effort to explore Mars. NASA has already built and tested the spacecraft and instruments that will be used in future Martian missions. One day in the not-too-distant future, we may know almost as much about Mars as we do about our home planet. Such knowledge could one day lead to landing humans on that distant planet.

Exploration of the unique and beautiful Martian landscape will become more common in the years ahead.

INDEX